# Whore

## A Swear Word Coloring Book
## For Release Anger

By

# S.B. Nozaz

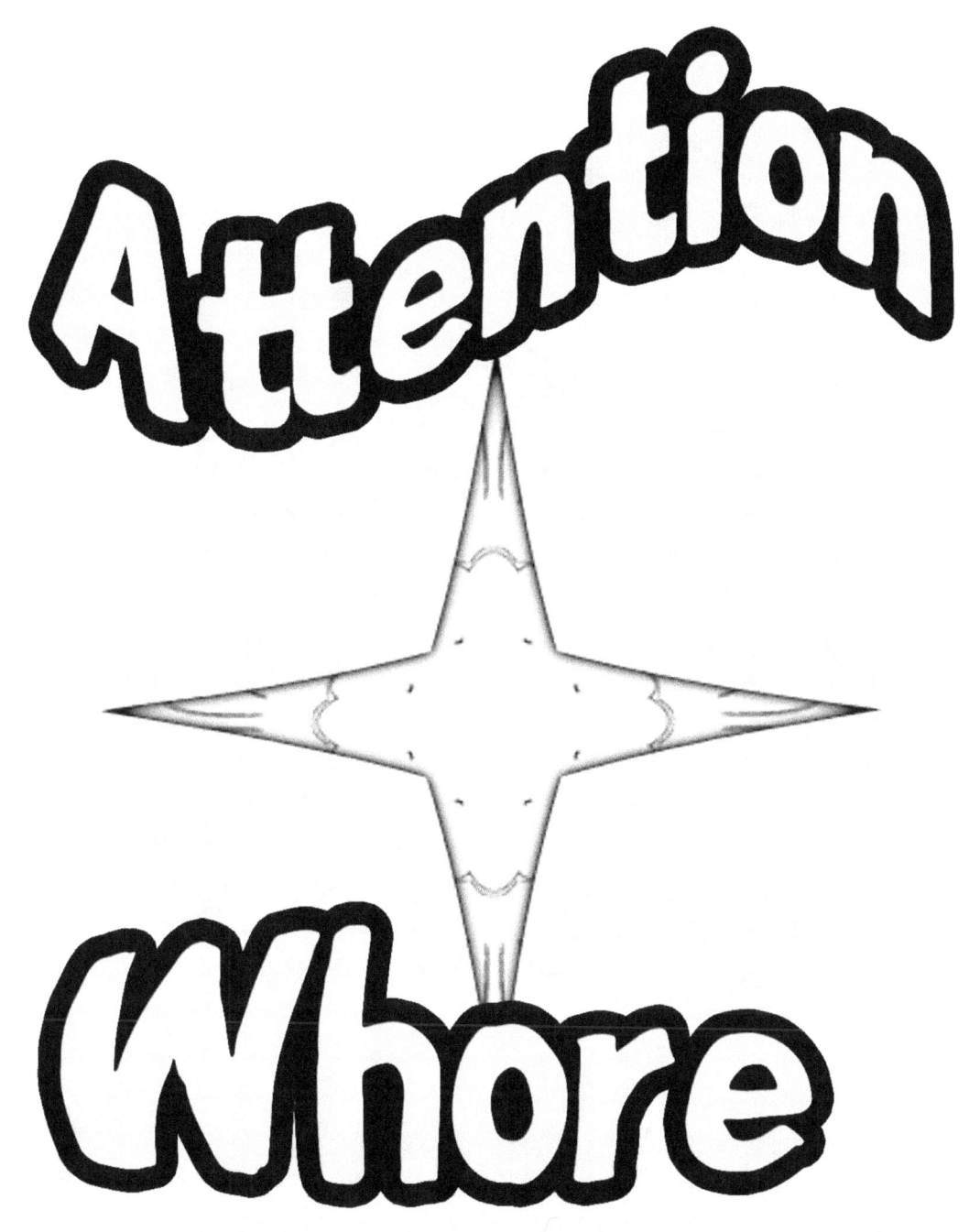

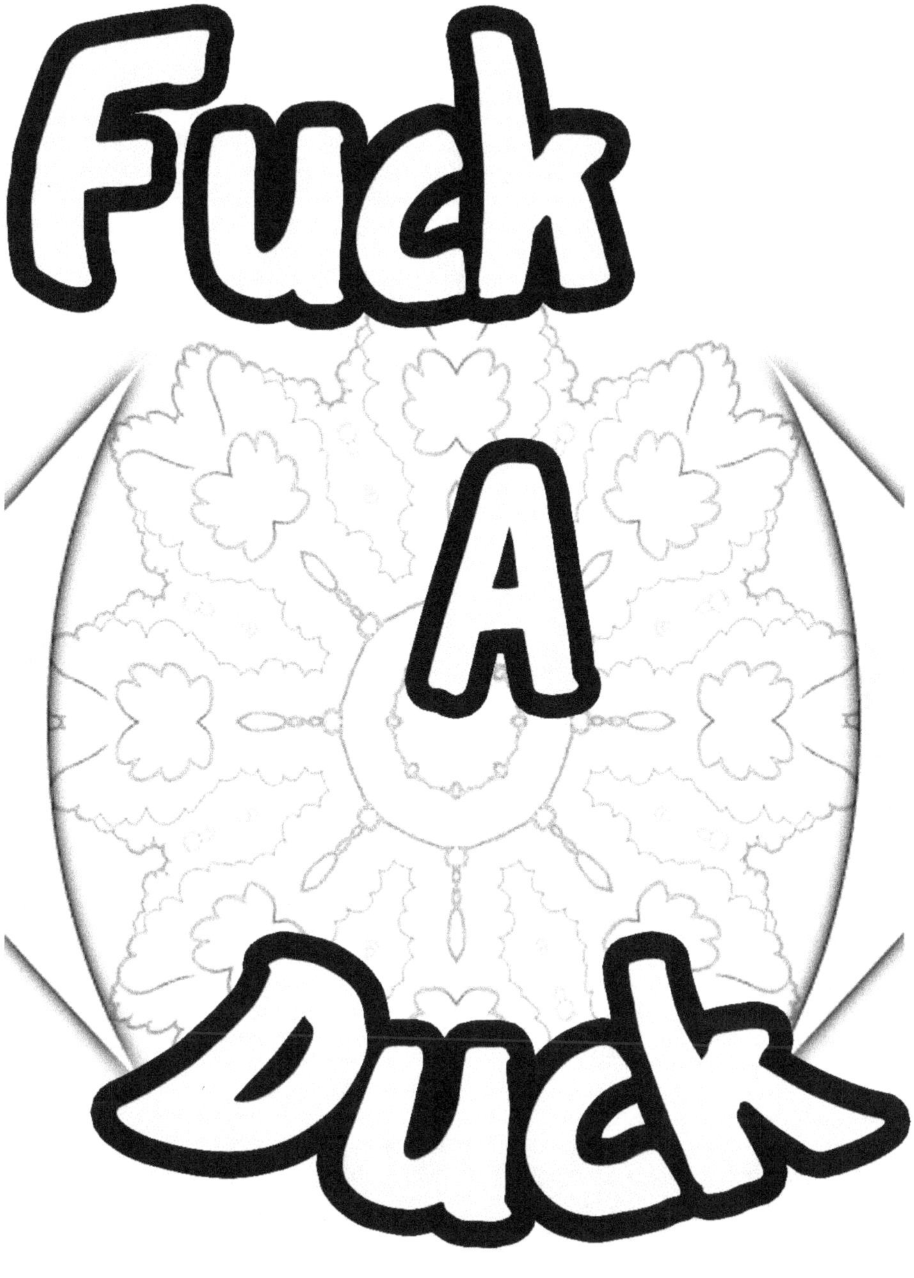
Fuck
A
Duck

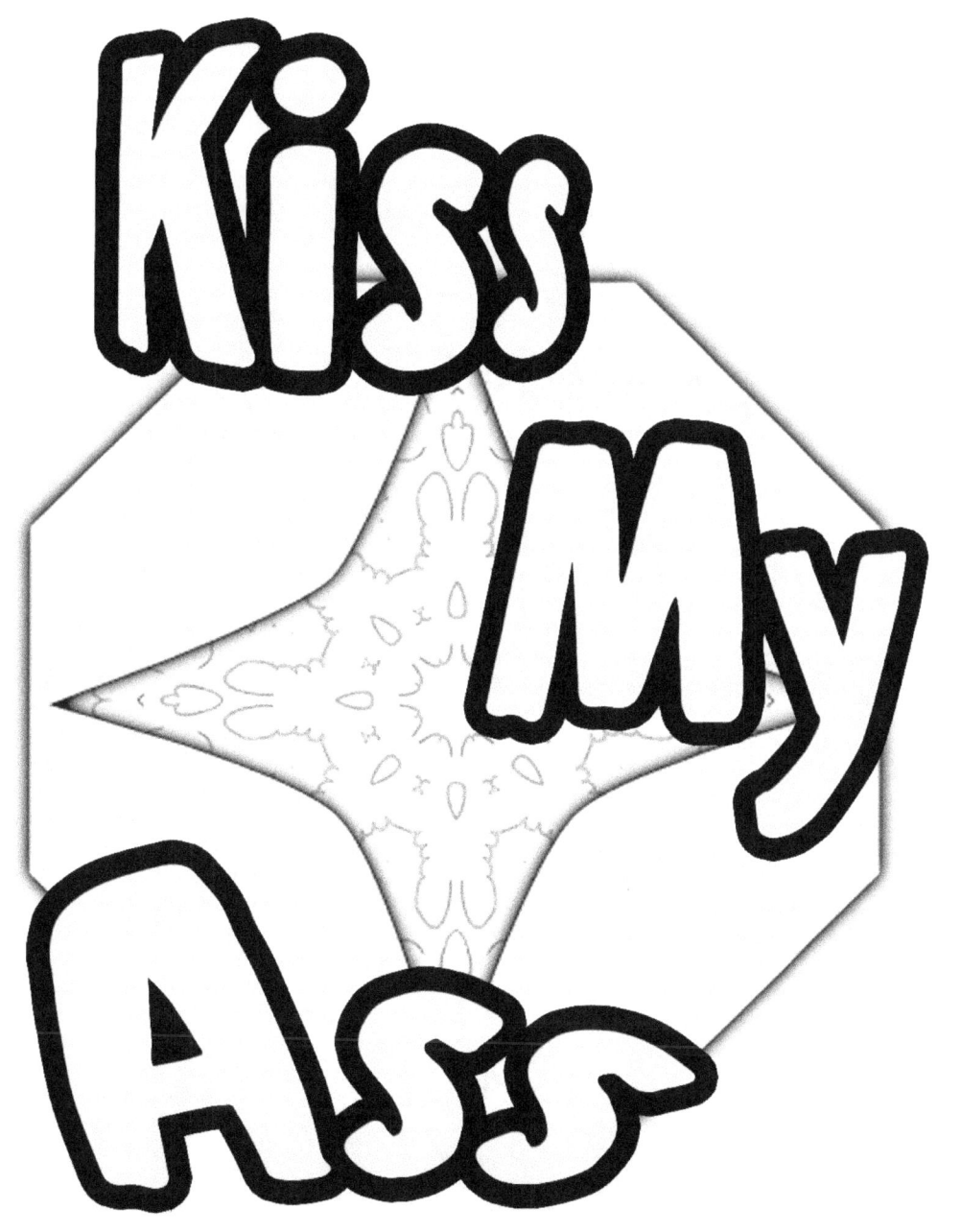

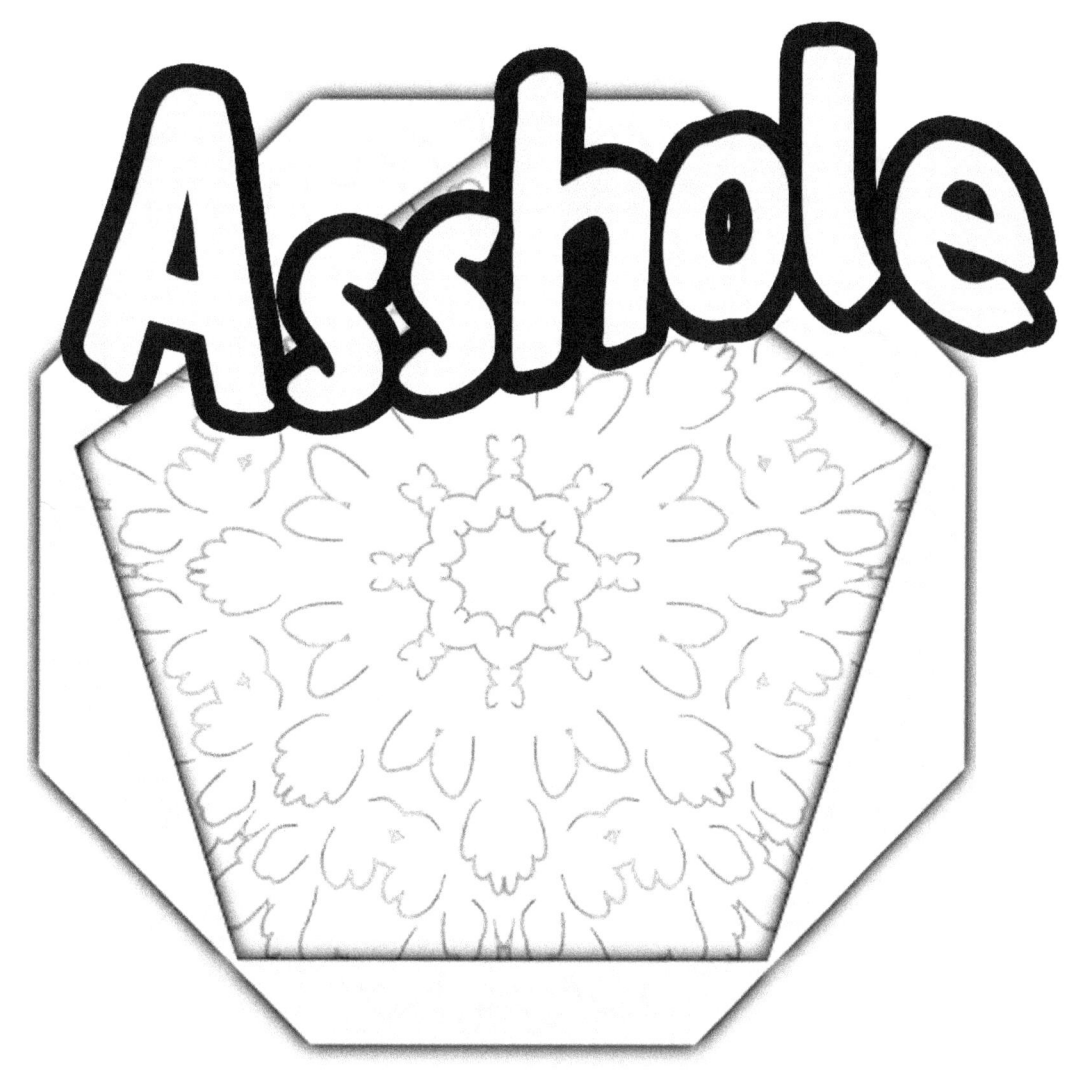

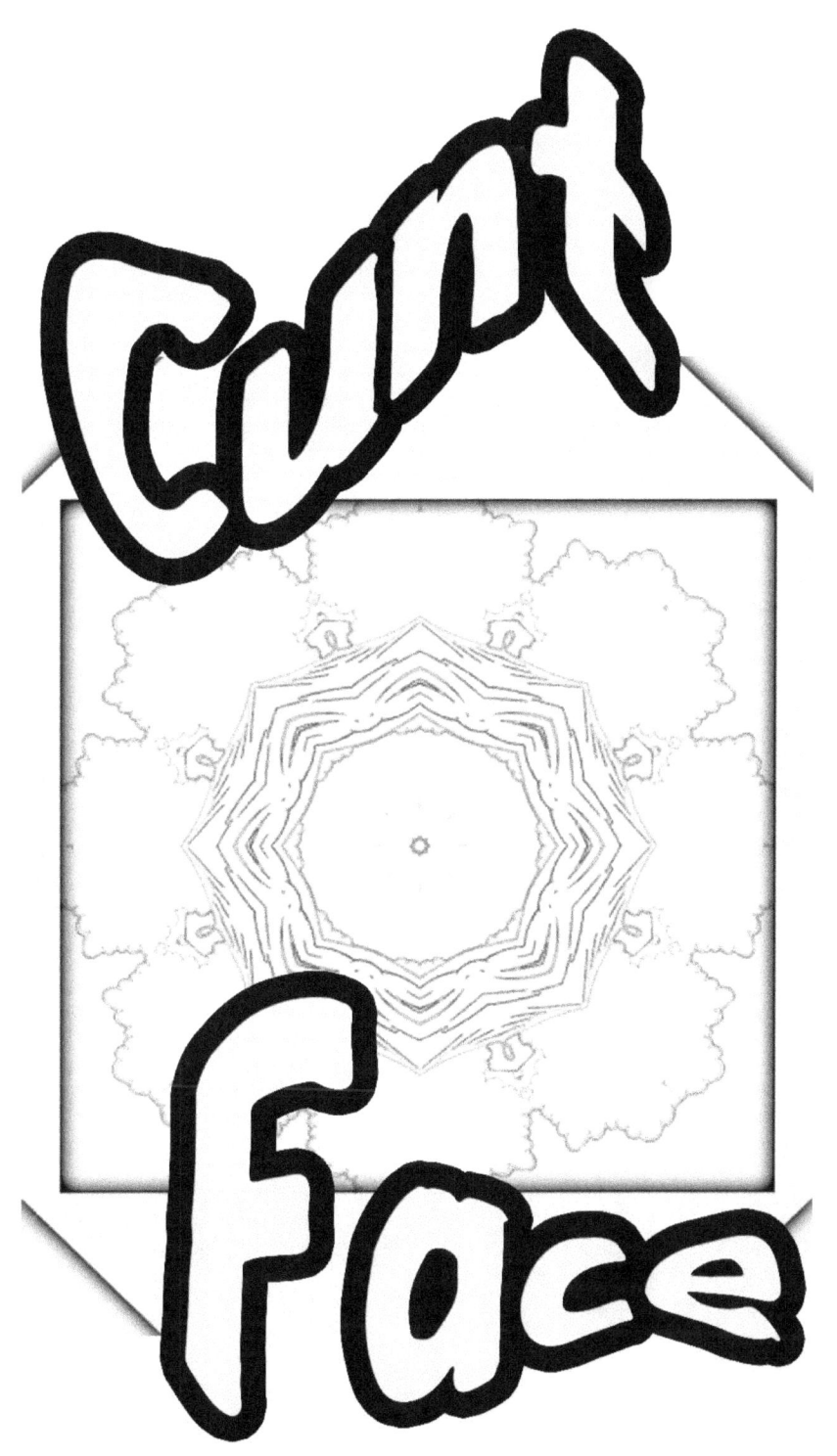

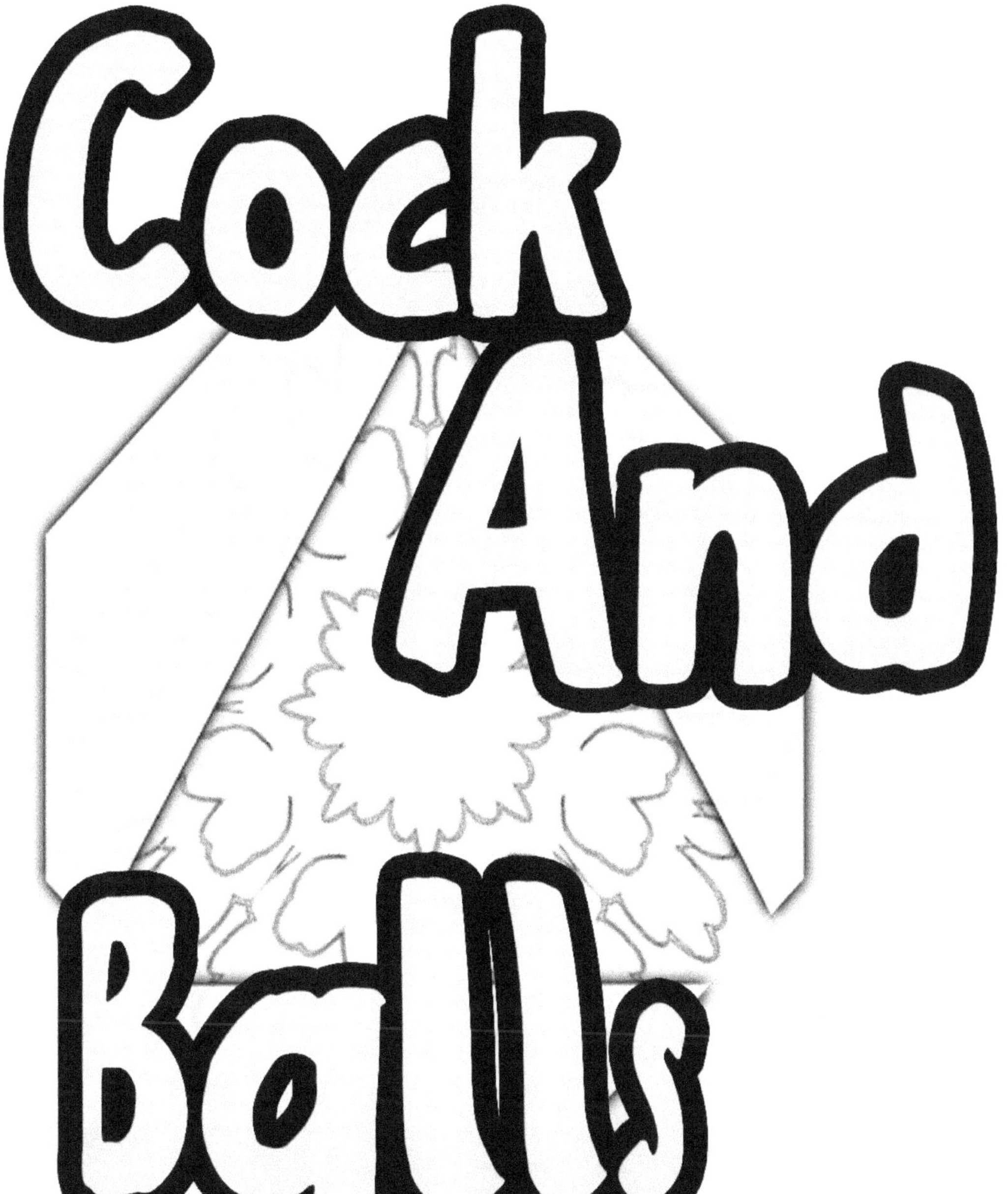
Cock
And
Balls

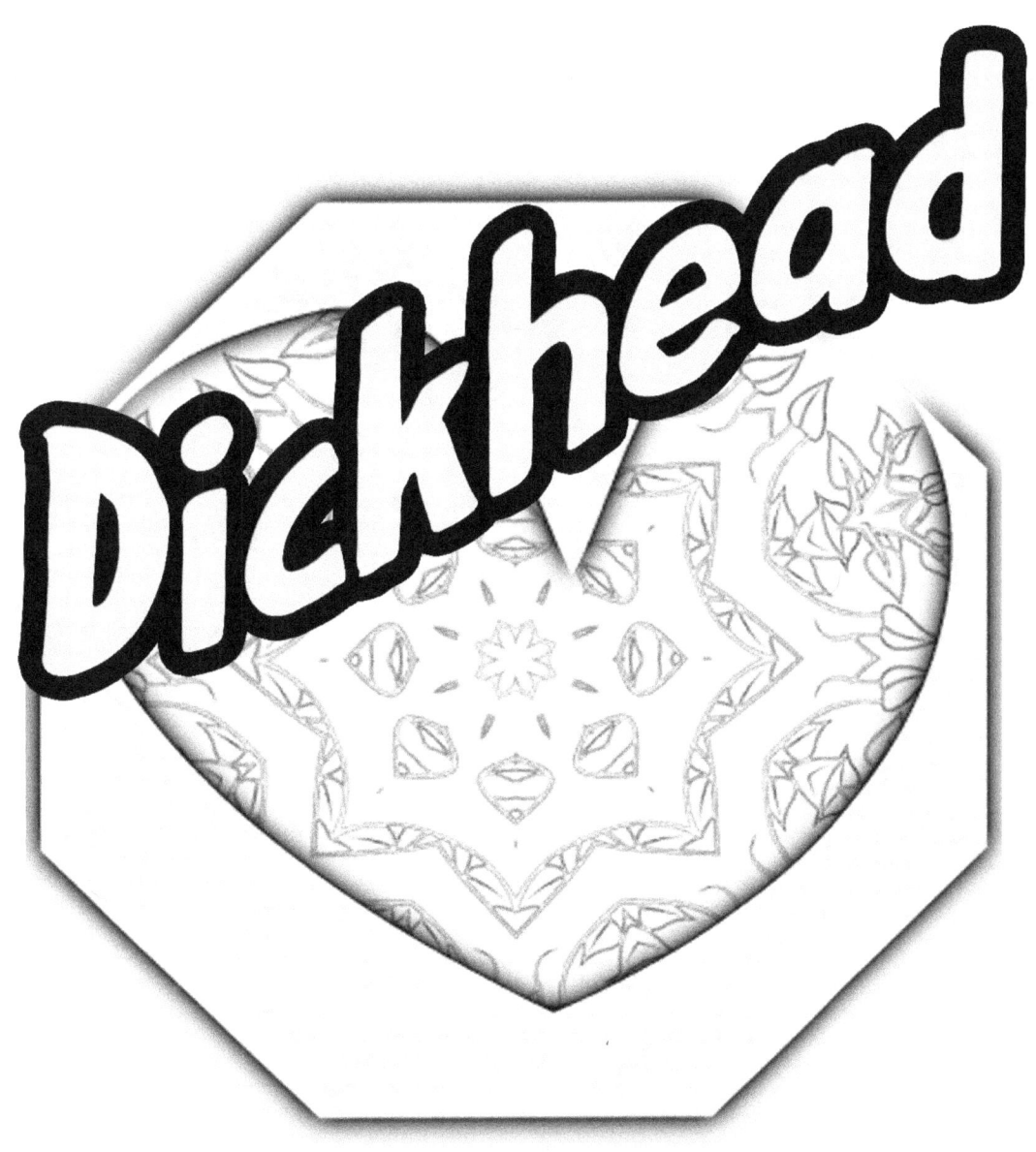

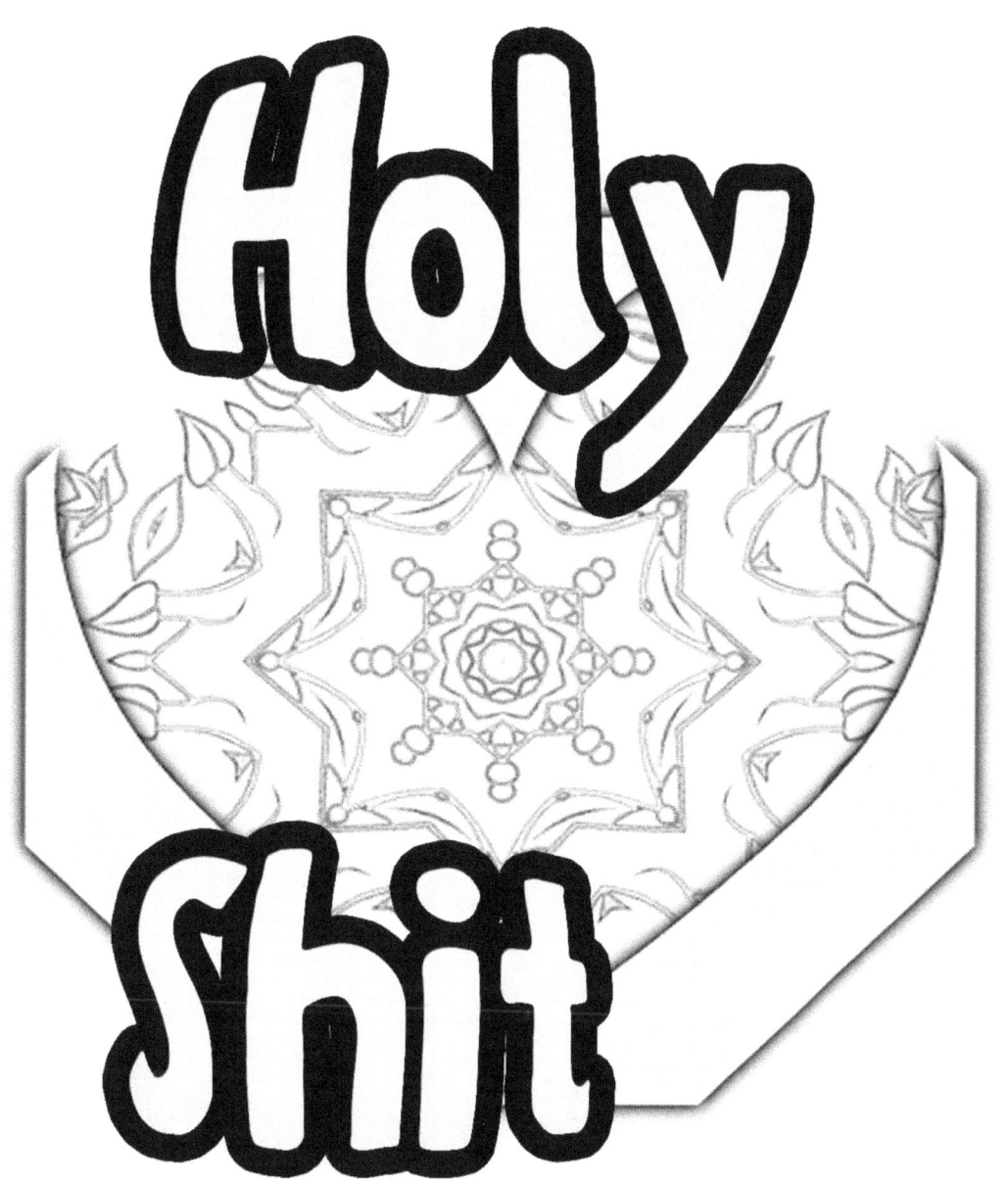

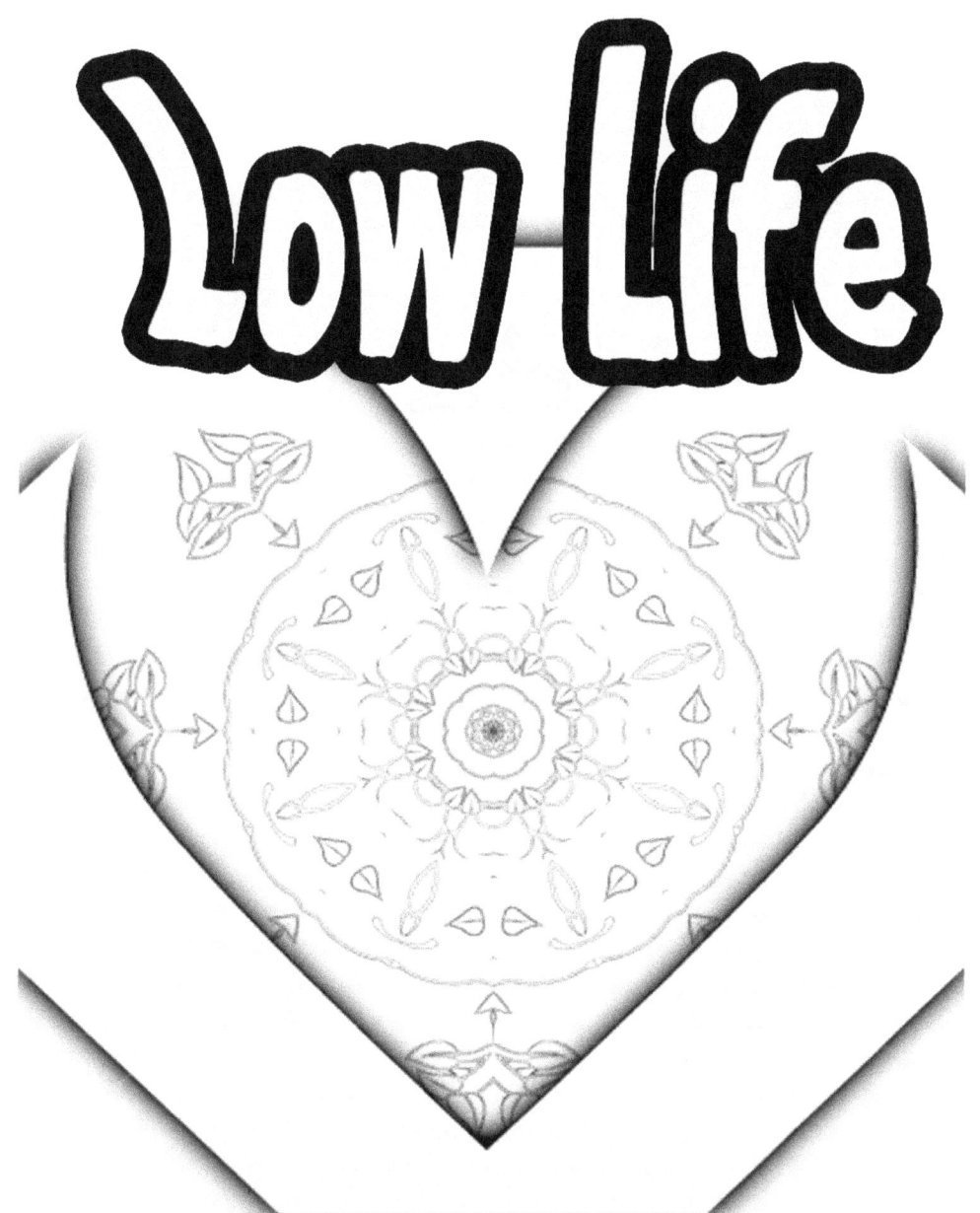

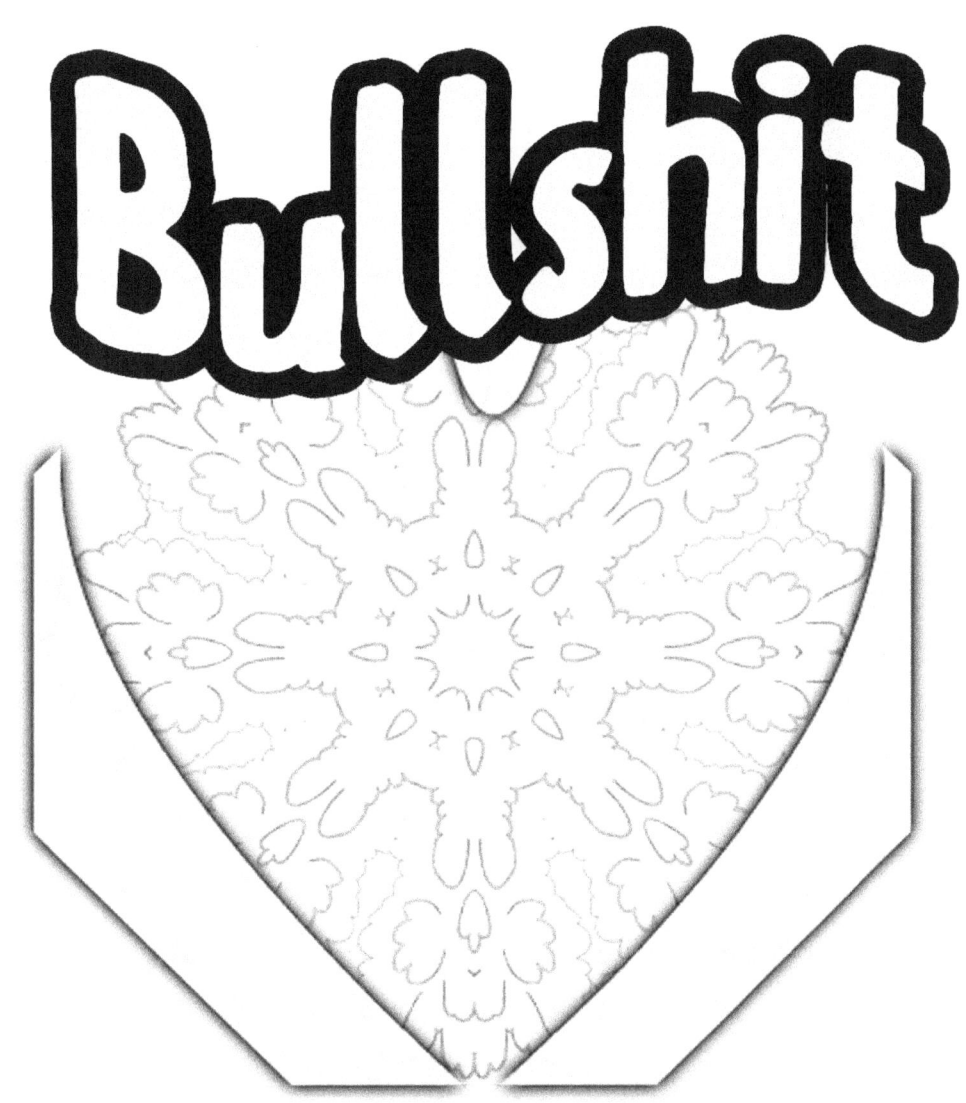

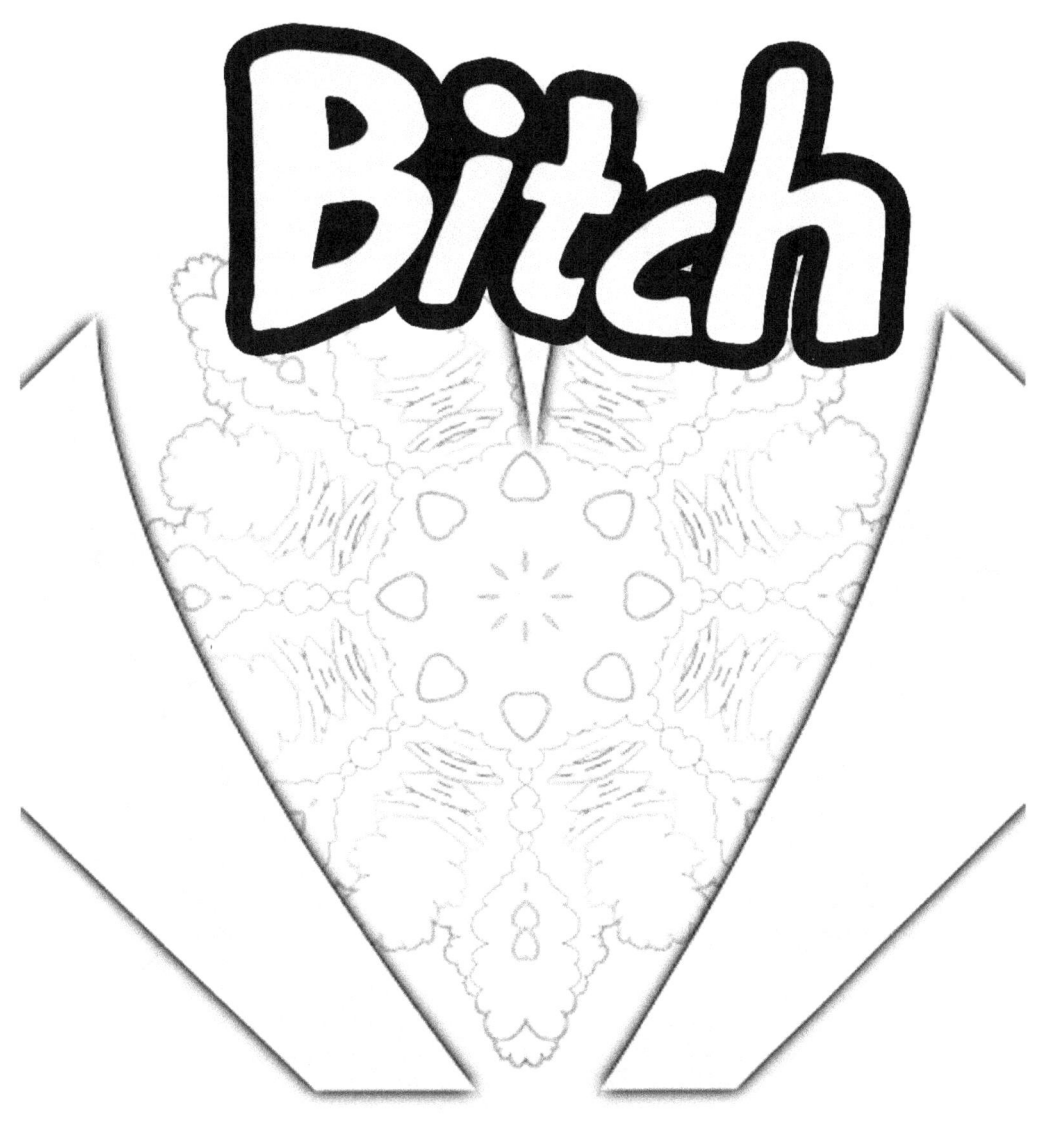

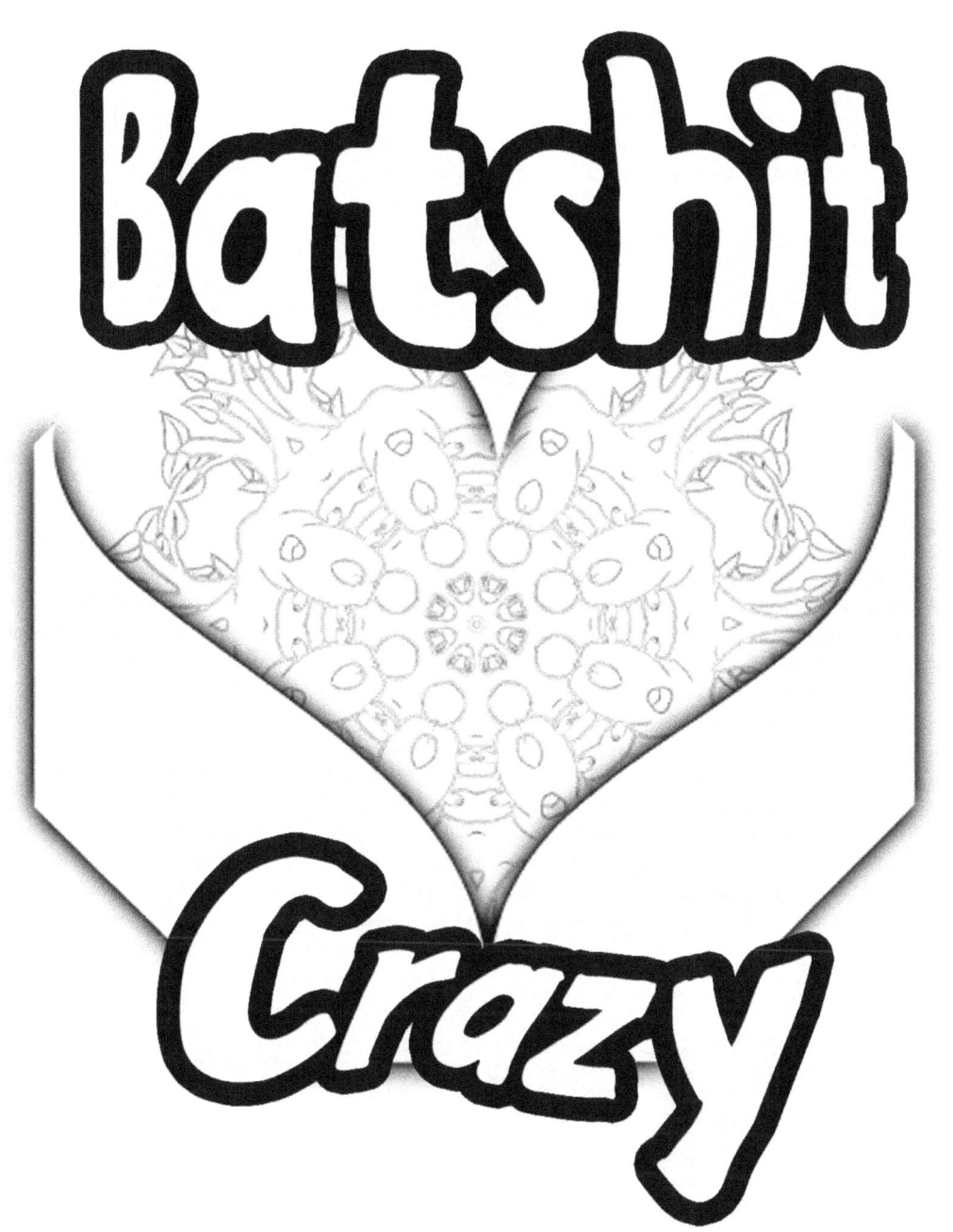

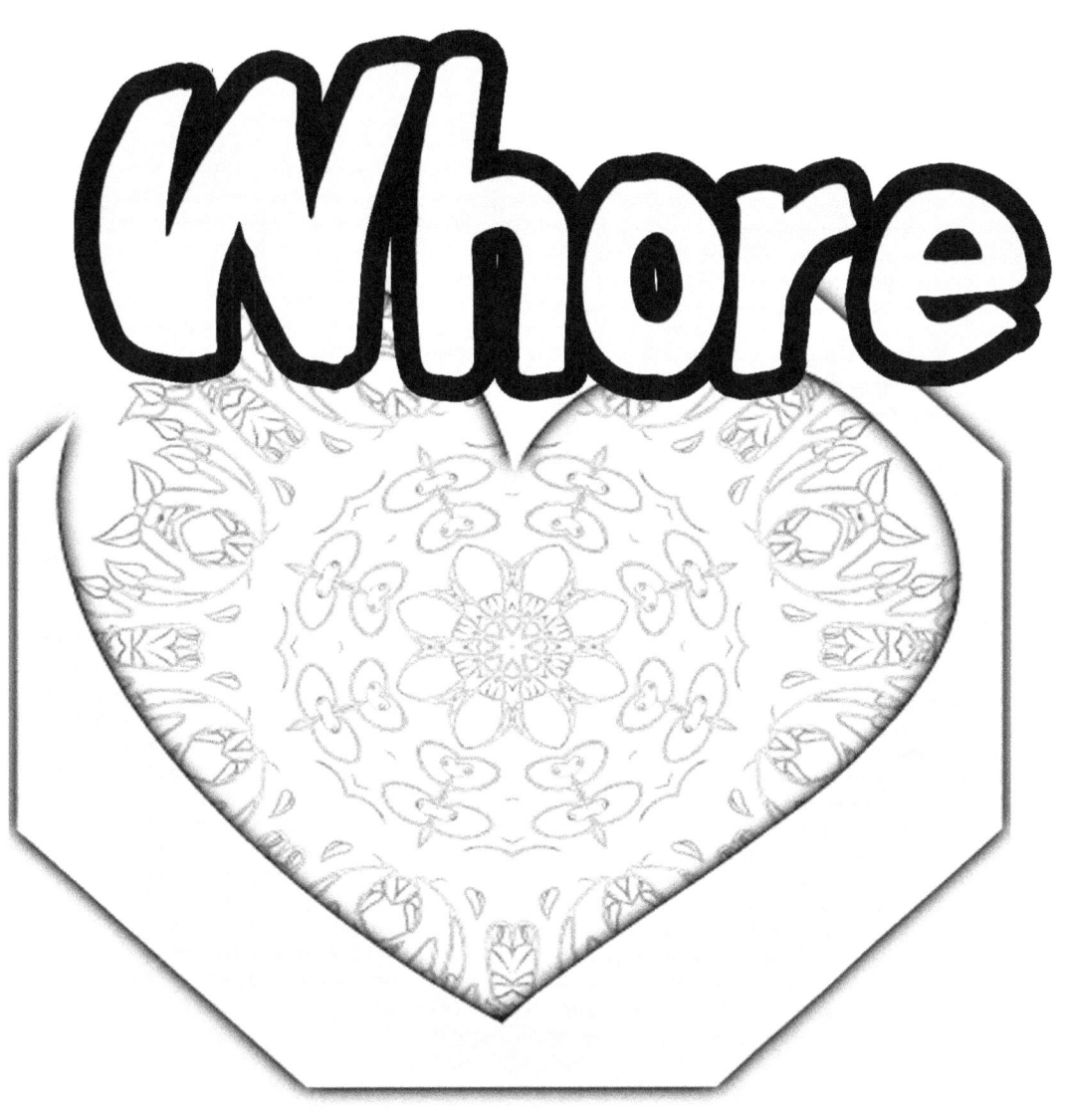

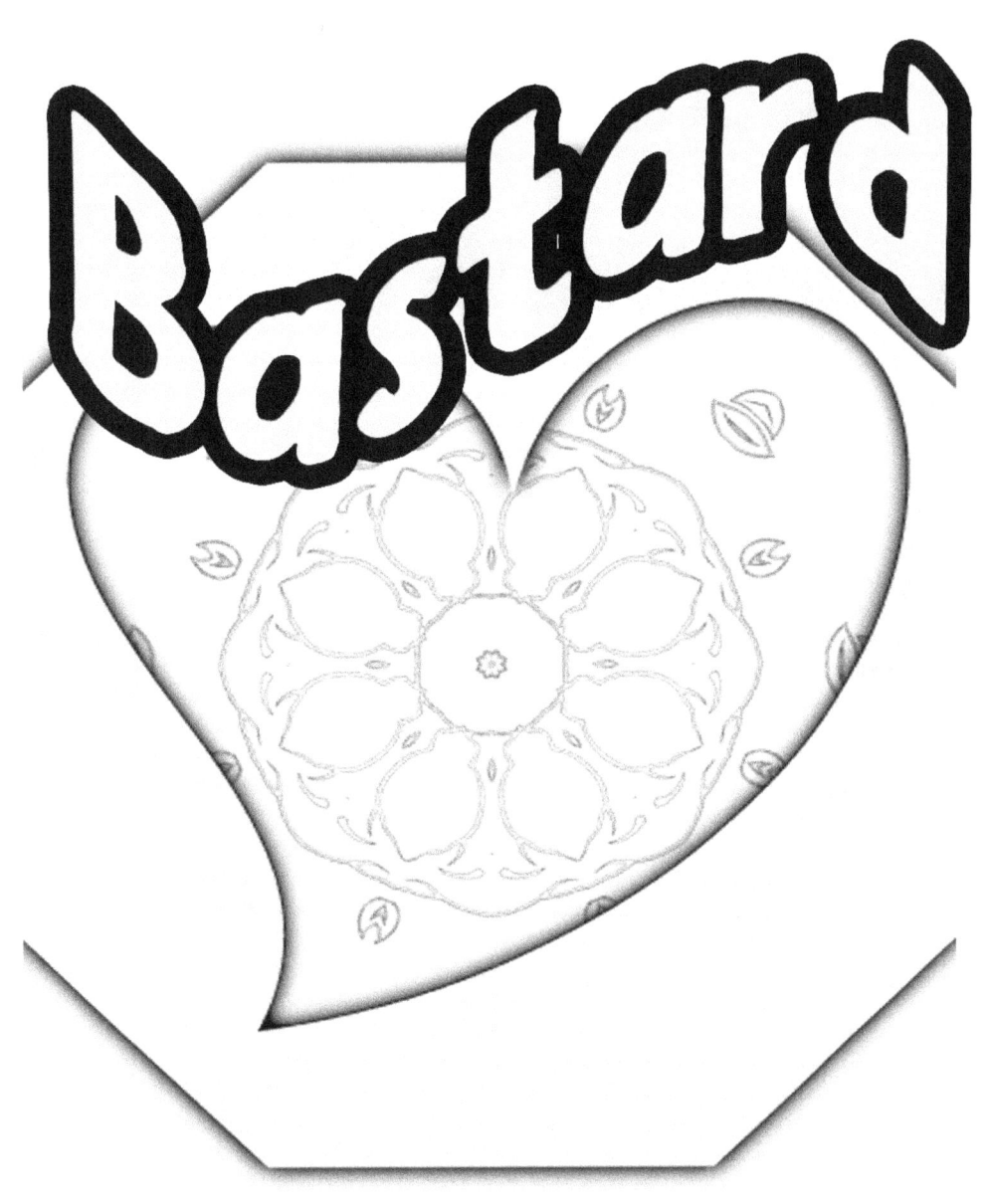

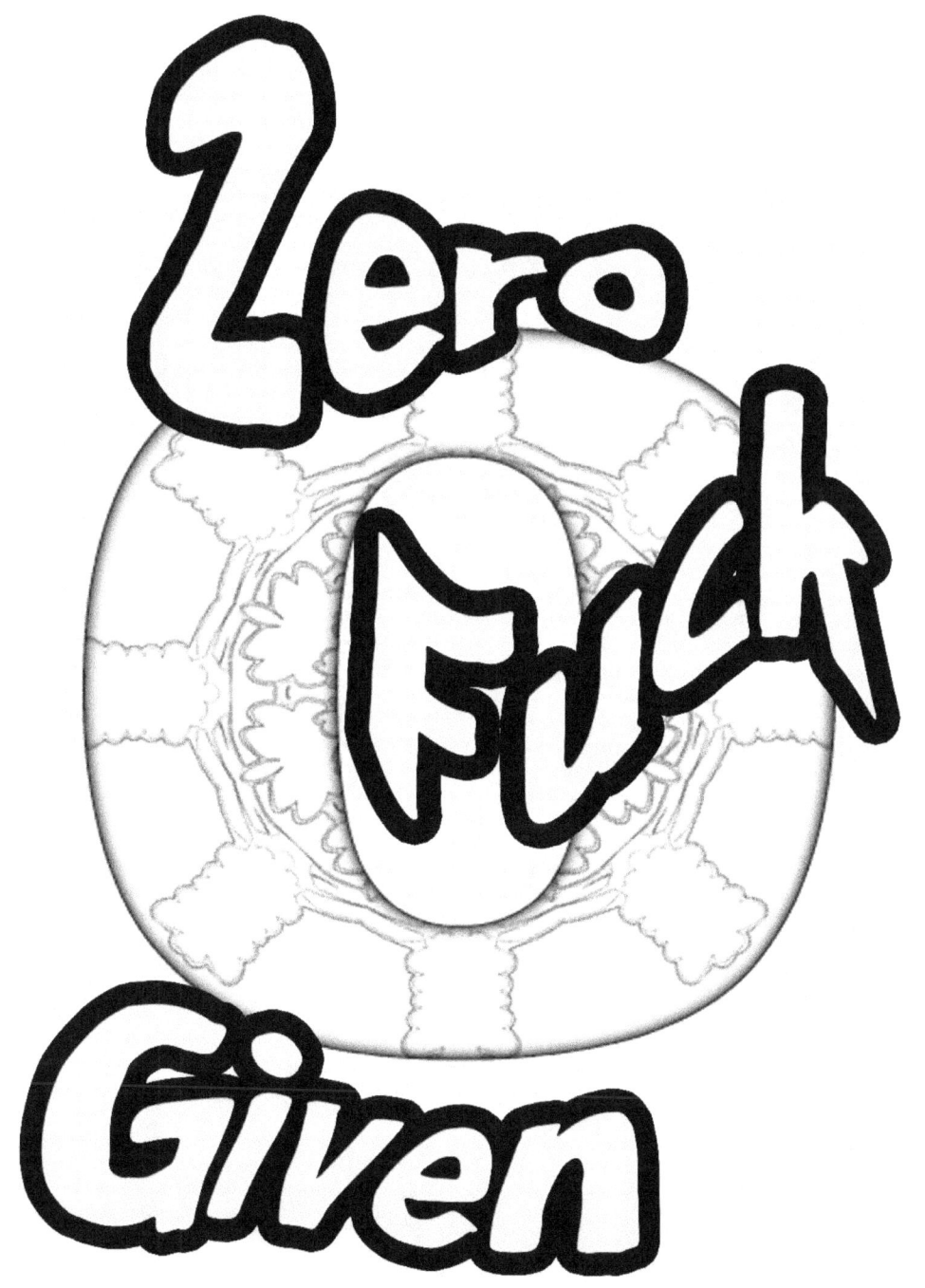

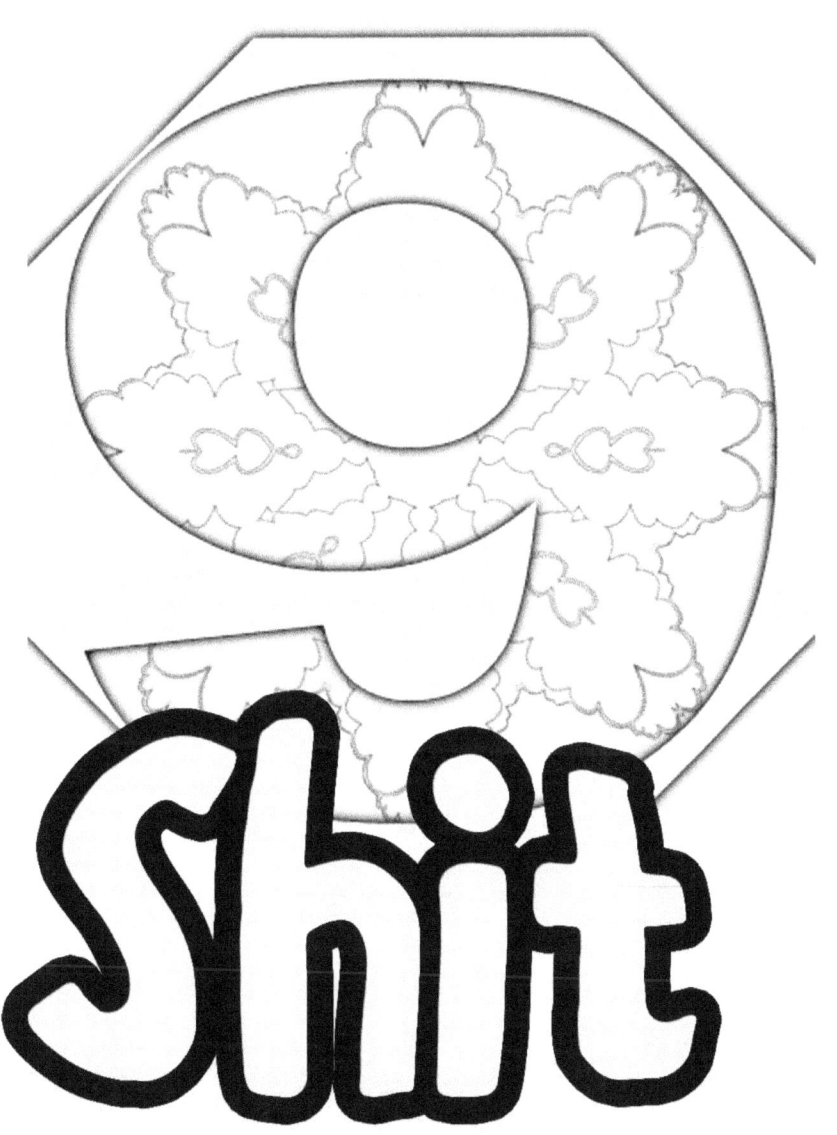

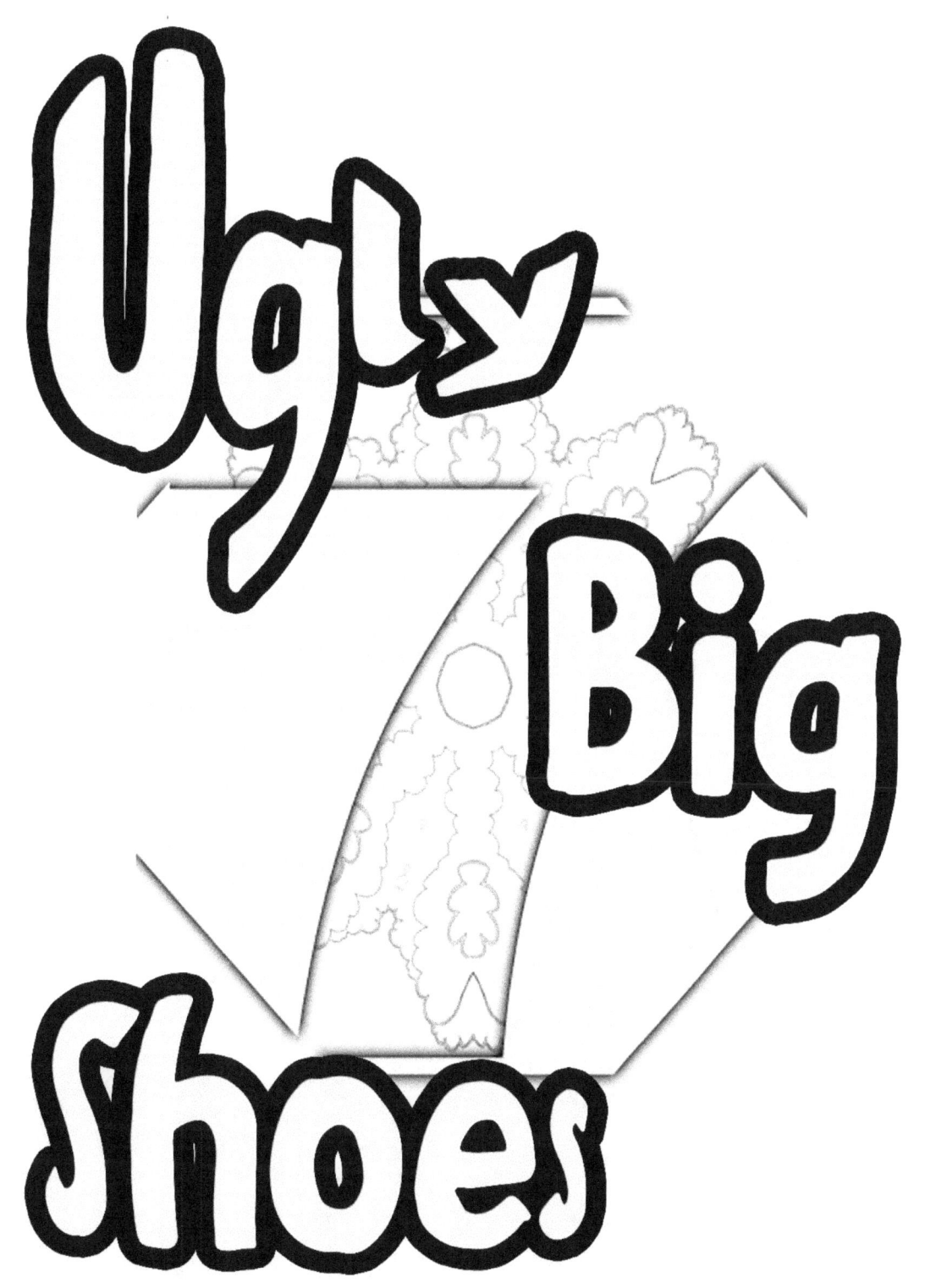

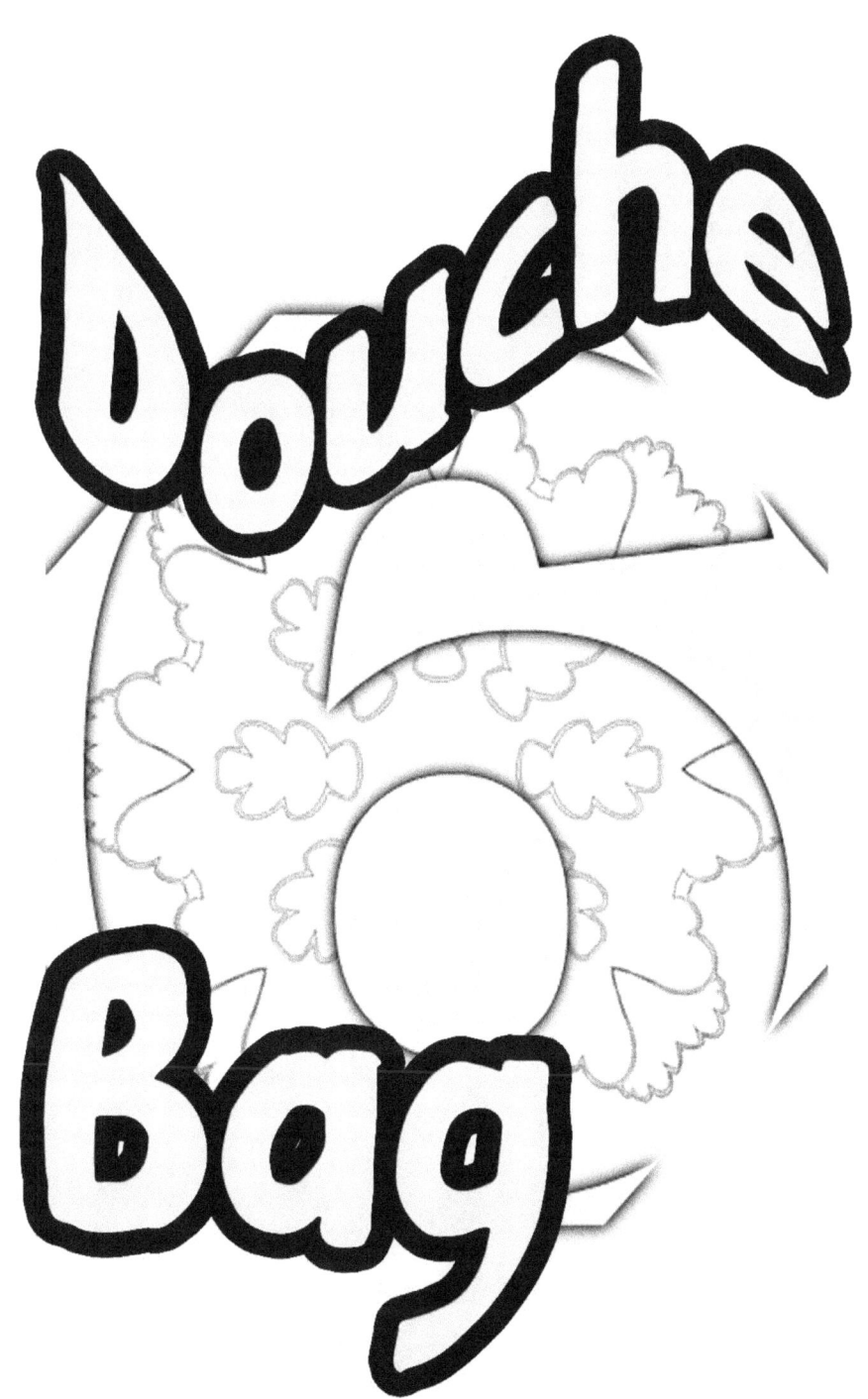

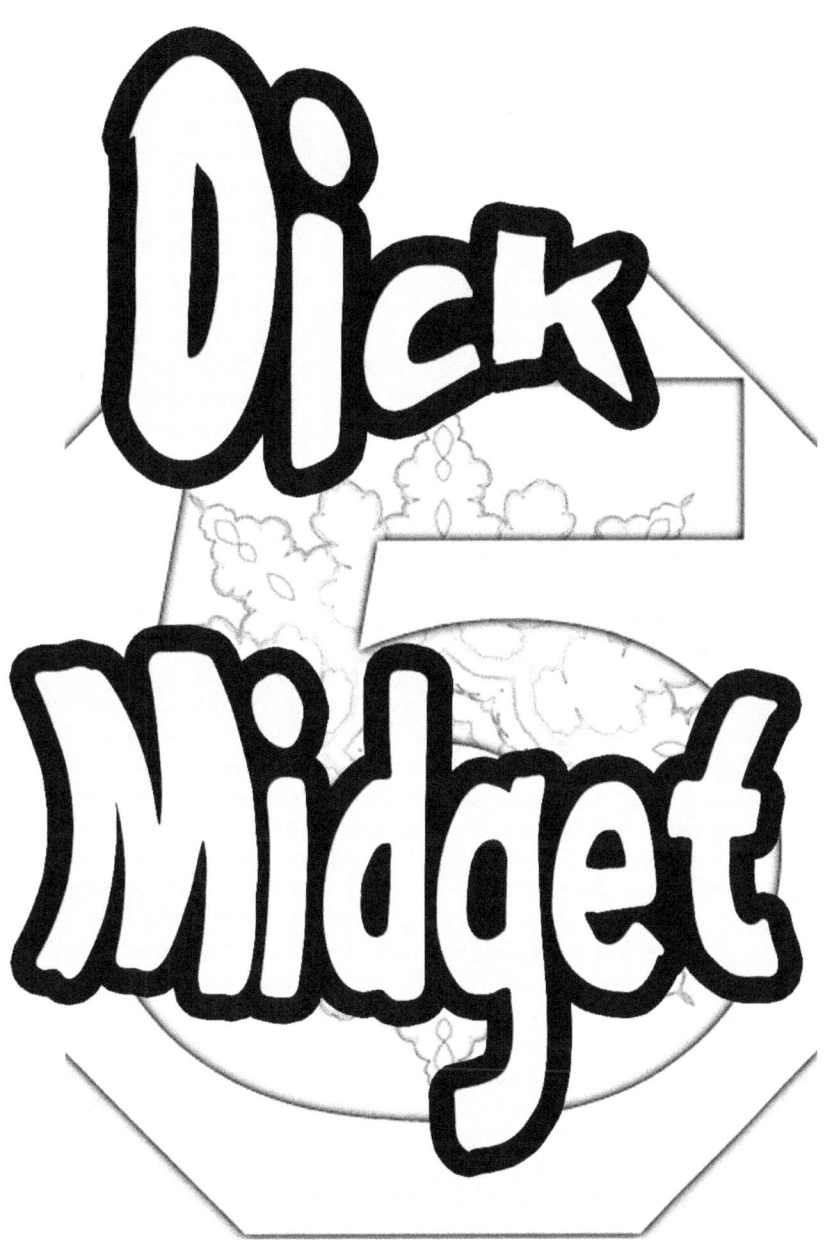

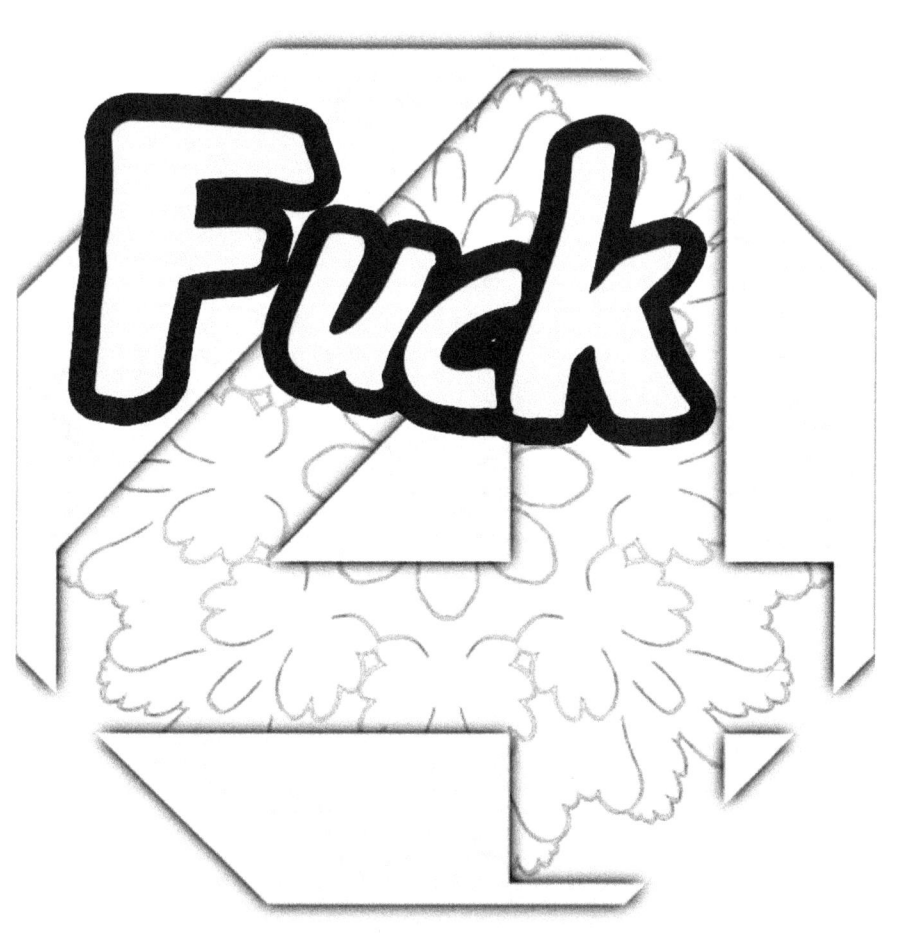

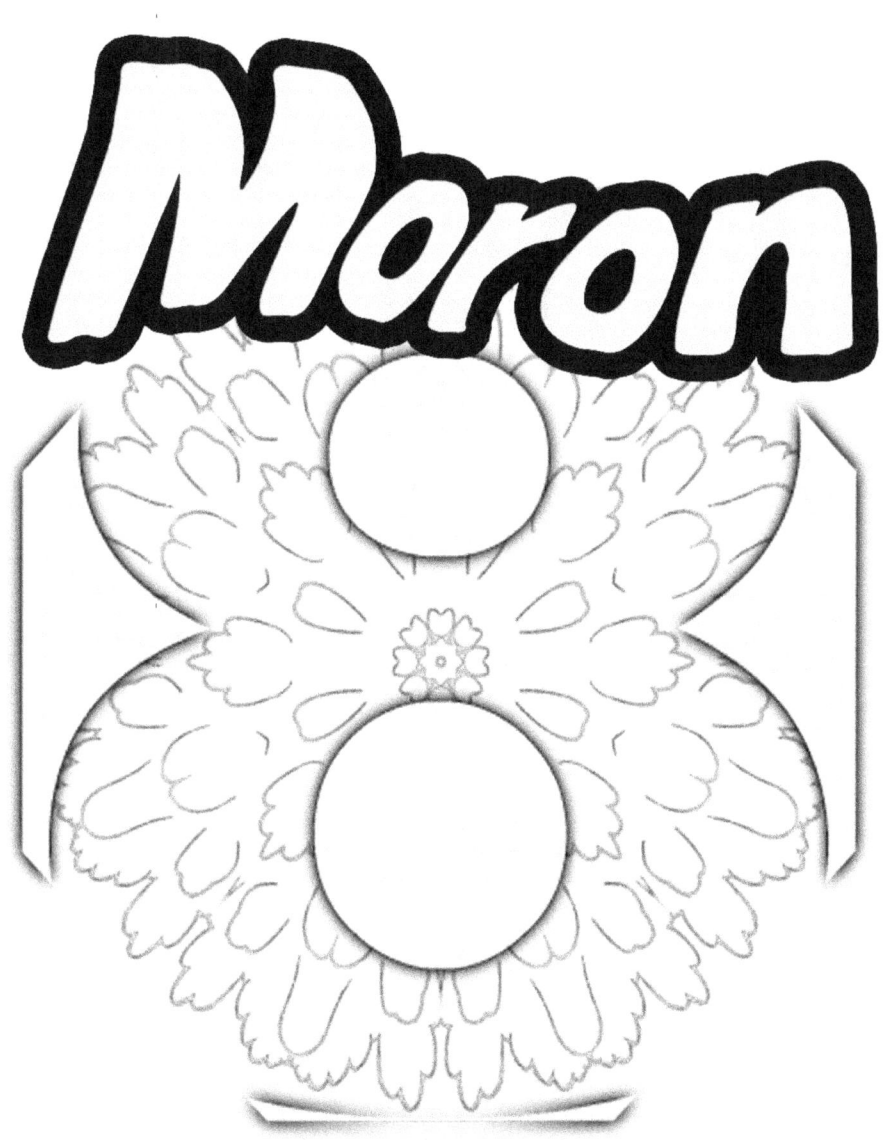

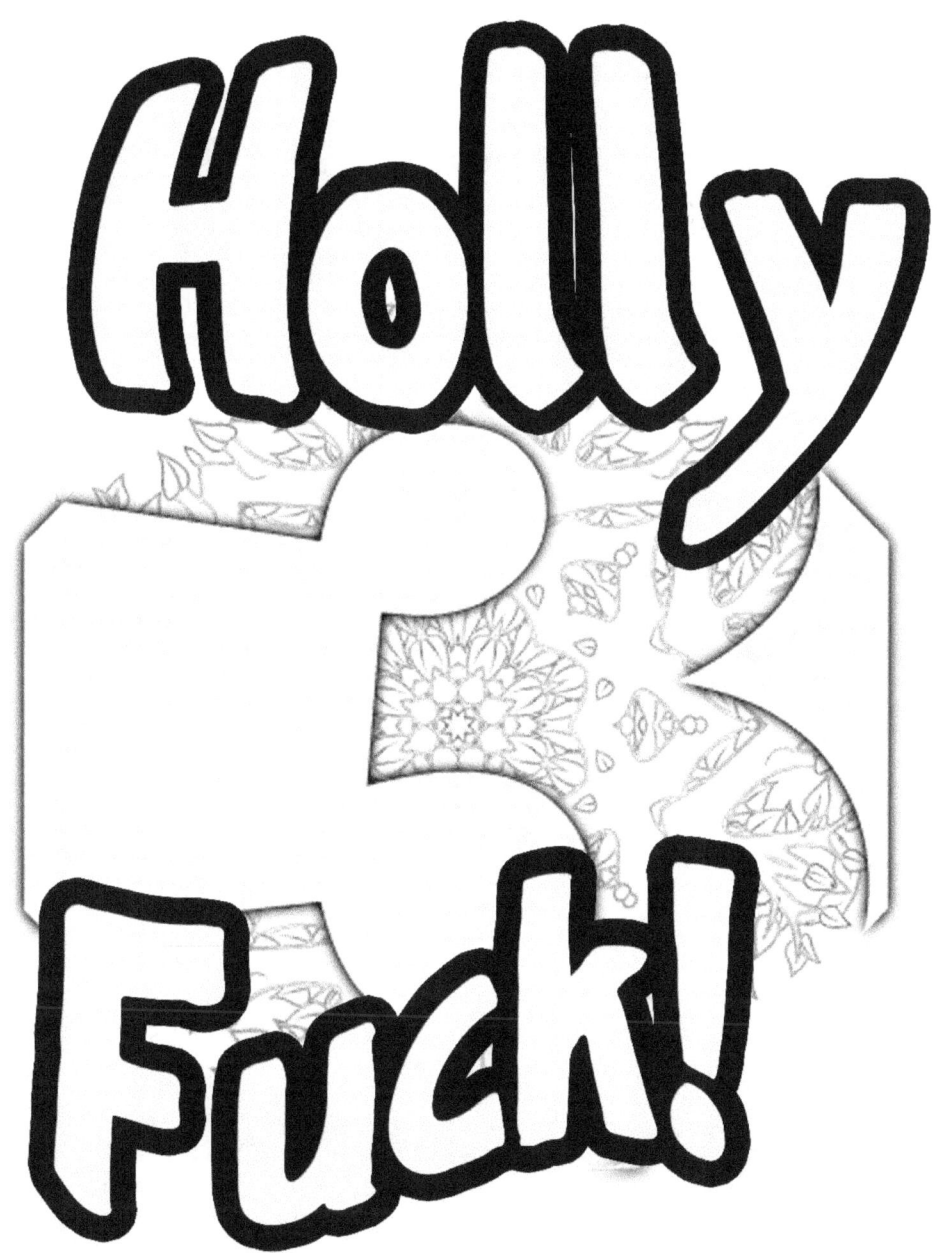

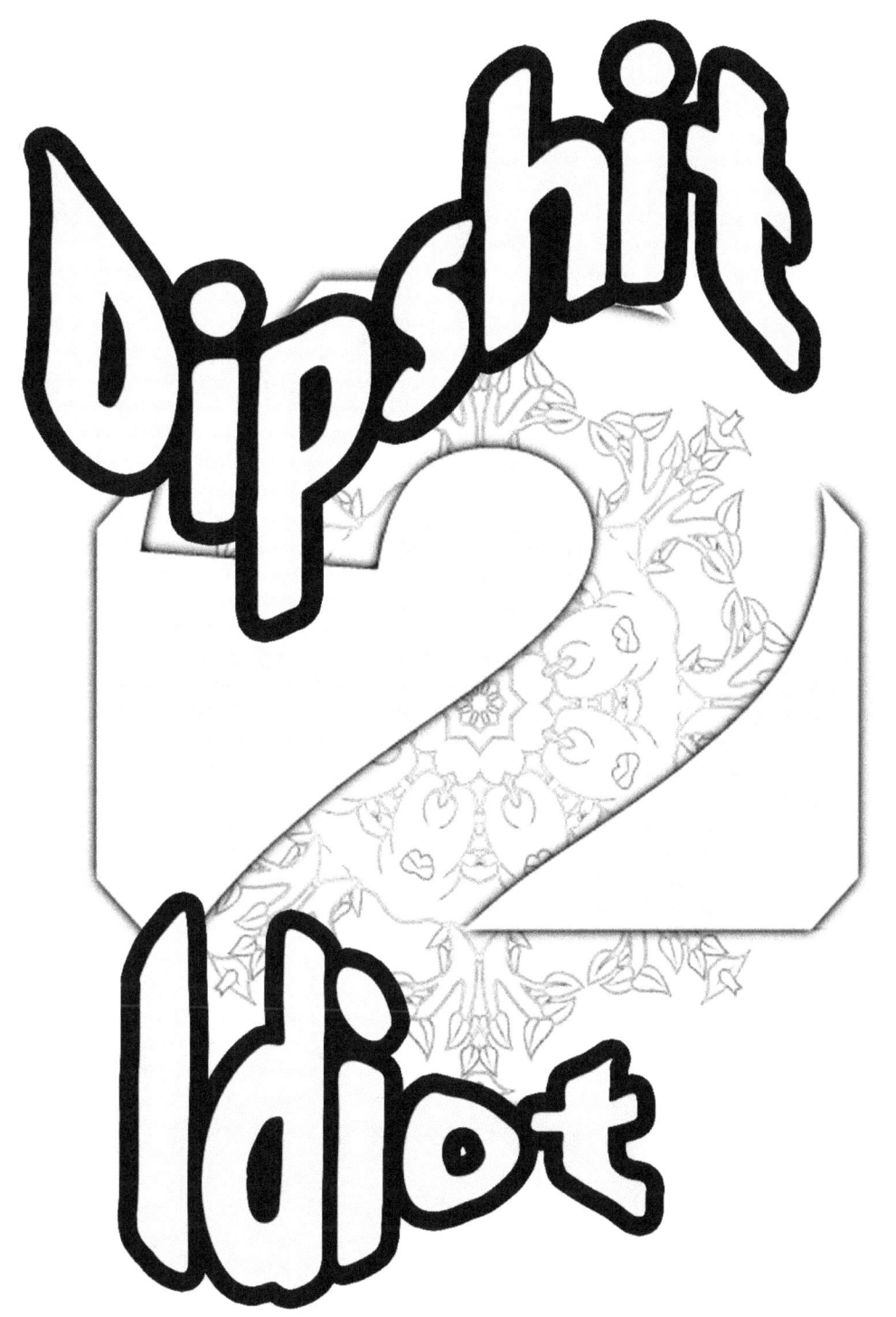

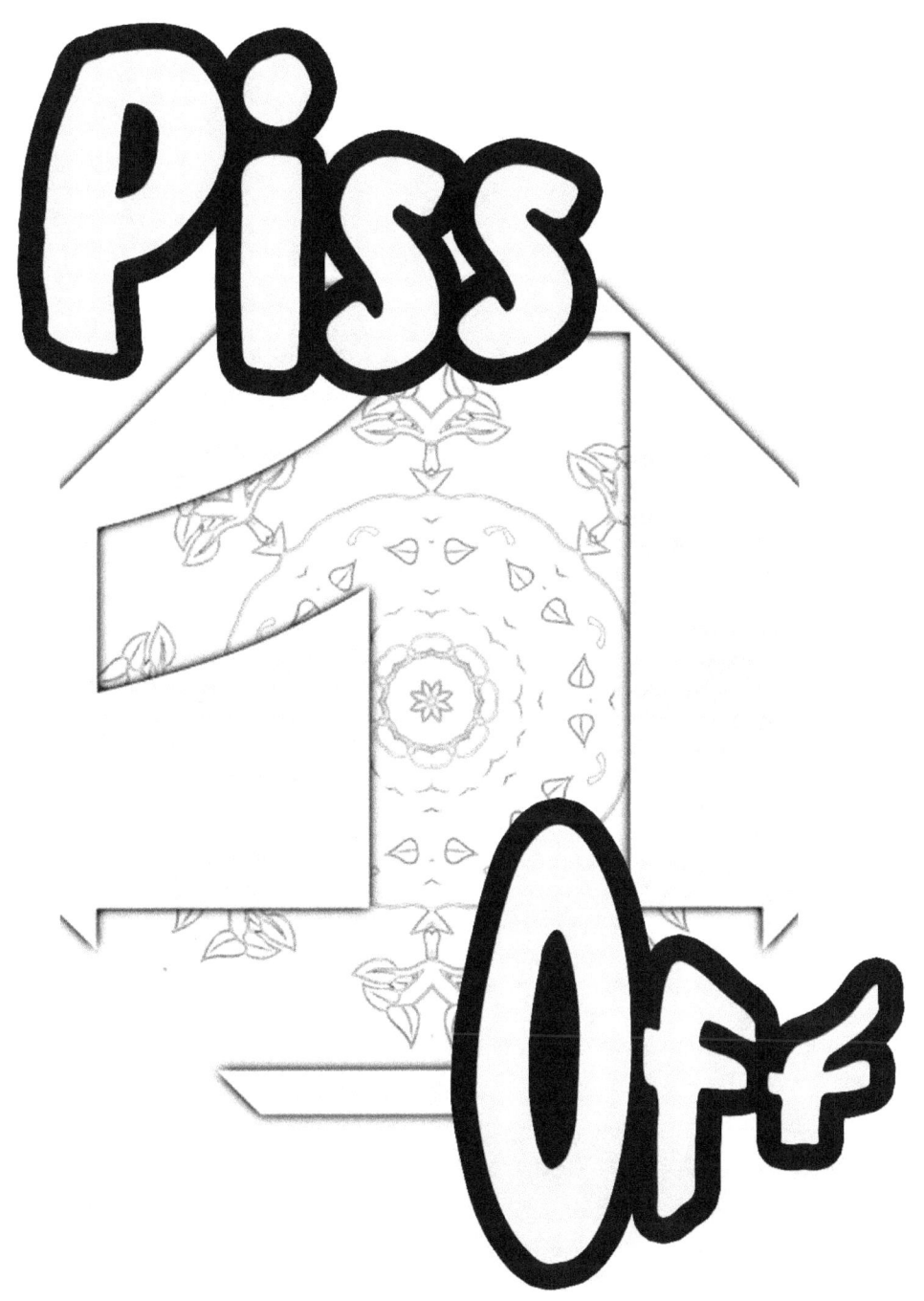

# Note

www.ingramcontent.com/pod-product-compliance
Lightning Source LLC
Chambersburg PA
CBHW080635190526
45169CB00009B/3403